No part of this book may be scanned, reproduced or distributed in any printed or electronic form without the prior permission of the author or publisher.

Dear ....

This gift is for you because…

....
....
....
....
....
....

Month ....
Year ....

APPRECIATION

Let us be grateful to those people that make us happy: they are the charming gardeners who make our souls blossom.

Marcel Proust

You are special to me because...

One of my fondest moments with you has been…

....

....

....

....

....

....

If I was to list five of your special qualities they would be...

1. ....

2. ....

3. ....

4. ....

5. ....

LOVE, FRIENDSHIP, LAUGHTER...SOME OF THE BEST THINGS IN LIFE REALLY ARE FREE.

— BOB MARLEY

THIS IS SOMETHING THAT YOU SAID THAT MEANS A LOT TO ME...

You were there for me..

"WE DON'T REMEMBER DAYS; WE REMEMBER MOMENTS"

CESARE PAVESE 1908 – 1950

You were so kind when.....

....

....

....

....

....

you make me smile......

....
....
....
....

A special celebration that I fondly remember sharing with you was...

Share your story and location

>>>————————————<<<

....

....

....

....

....

....

....

....

>>>————————————<<<

> "YOU WILL FIND, AS YOU LOOK BACK UPON LIFE, THAT THE MOMENTS THAT STAND OUT ARE THE MOMENTS WHEN YOU HAVE DONE THINGS FOR OTHERS."

HENRY DRUMMOND (1851 - 1897)

you do this better than anyone else...

"Sometimes the heart see's what is invisable to the eye"

H. Jackson Brwon. JR.

If there was one word to describe you, it would be..

SHARE YOUR STORY

I always smile when I think of this story...

ADD A PHOTO HERE

A Special Moment Together

More Special Moments Together

> The meaning of life is to find your gift. The purpose of life is to give it away
>
> *Pablo Picasso*

I want to conclude this by saying...

....

....

....

....

....

....

....

....

....

NOTES

BOOKS IN THE THANK YOU. SERIES

Thank You For Being the Best Dad
Thank You For Being the Best Papa
Thank You For Being the Best Mom
Thank You For Being the Best Mum
Thank You For Being the Best Sister
Thank You For Being the Best Brother
Thank You For Being the Best Cousin
Thank You For Being the Best Grandmother
Thank You For Being the Best Grandfather
Thank You For Being the Best Pa
Thank You For Being the Best Nana
Thank You For Being the Best Nonna
Thank You For Being the Best Uncle
Thank You For Being the Best Aunt
Thank You For Being a Great Teacher
Thank You For Being a Great Coach
Thank You For Being a Great Friend
Thank You For Being a Great Doctor

AVAILABLE IN ALL MAJOR BOOKSTORES

www.ingramcontent.com/pod-product-compliance
Lightning Source LLC
LaVergne TN
LVHW070213080526
838202LV00063B/6597